A very NEW WAY of getting children to sleep!

EASTER IN RAMALLAH

By Wafa Shami

Illustrated by Shaima Farouki

ISBN: 978-0-9600147-3-6
      0-9600147-3-X

Library of Congress In-Publication Data
Shami, Wafa
1. Children Fiction Books 2. Christian 3. Multi-Cultural

Illustrations by Shaima' Farouki
Copywrite office: Certificate of Registration TX u 2-112-737
Registration August 16, 2019

Printed in the United States of America

To my sweet little boy Faris, I love you more than words can say.

It was a sunny and beautiful spring day in Ramallah and Noor loved to sit in the sun. She loved the feel of the warm sun brushing her face and warming her small body. Mama always worried. She would call out to her from the window:

"Don't sit so long in the sun, you will get a head-ache!" But Noor didn't care. She continued to lie on the grass.

The feel of the warm sun, the silence, the smell of the flowers and blooming of the fruit trees in dad's backyard gave the place a magical feel and eight-year-old Noor felt like she owned the place.

oor's best friend was her next-door neighbor, Laila.

They were both eight years old. Laila would often come to Noor's backyard and the two would talk and laugh. During spring they would pick green almonds from the tree and put them in the bowl Noor had brought from the kitchen.

They would sprinkle salt on the almonds then sit under the almond tree and enjoy the sour, salty taste of the almonds.

Now it was a week before Easter. Noor and her family, who were Christians, were observing Lent, abstaining from eating meat and dairy products during the 40 days before Easter Sunday. So Laila and Noor were discussing fasting and each one talking about her own family practices.

Laila, who was Muslim, said: "It's easier to fast from sunrise to sundown and then eat whatever we want all night, like we do during the month of Ramadan, it would be hard for me to fast from meat and dairy for 40 days."

"I think not eating and drinking all day is more difficult," argued Noor. "I can't imagine not eating chocolate or cheese every day for 40 days," Laila countered.

So argued the two girls while eating the salted almonds, which were one of their favorite food to eat in Spring.

It was Holy Week, the last week of Lent which ends with Easter Sunday, Noor's favorite holiday. Noor loved to go to church with her family to attend Mass on Thursday and Friday before Easter.

The Good Friday Mass was particularly exquisite. It's true that it started at 5:00 in the afternoon and was not over until 9:00 at night, and sometimes Noor would get bored. But still, it was one of the most beautiful masses that Noor had grown up attending. And she would not want to miss the excitment and the crowds of this occasion.

Then came Saturday and the Light Parade, which Noor also loved attending and had never missed a year.

This year, Noor and Laila went together to the parade, accompanied by Noor's older sister.

The Light Parade started at Al-Manara in the center of the city and circled around the main street. Clergymen led the parade. They carried long candles they had lit in the Church of the Holy Sepulcher in Jerusalem, and used them to light the smaller candles of the people lining the street on both sides of the procession.

Noor and Laila held their candles up high toward the clergyman. He smiled at the two sweet girls when he lit their candles.

eating their drums and playing their bagpipe, marching bands of girl and boy scouts followed behind clergymen. Noor's favorite band was Siriyet Ramallah.

"The moment I hear their rhythm, my heart beats with excitement," Noor told Laila.

As the parade reached its end point at the Greek Orthodox Church, Laila exclaimed, "Oh it was amazing!"

Another exciting thing about Saturday was that after the parade, as she did every year, Noor returned home to color Easter eggs with her mother.

Noor's mom had already gathered onionskins, fennel roots, red cabbage, and beets to make colors to dye the eggs. When the eggs were all colored and dry, Noor helped her mom put them neatly in the basket.

Earlier in the week Laila and her mother came over to help Noor's mom in making the special sweets for this holiday.

Ka'ek was a round cookie and stuffed with dates, and Ma'moul was stuffed with nuts and had the shape of a dome.

The smell of freshly baked Ka'ek and ma'moul cookies made from semolina and butter especially for Easter—filled the kitchen, as Noor's mom took them out of the oven.

Noor ate a cookie and burned her tongue. "Ouch!" she cried out. "See? I told you to wait for them to cool off," said her mother, as she gave Noor a glass of water.

"Thank you, Mama, you were right, I'm sorry. But they are yummy!"

*F*inally, Easter Sunday was here! Noor got up in the morning and put on her new Easter dress, the colors of spring.

After greeting her parents, she went out to show off her dress to the neighborhood kids, her Easter eggs basket on her arm.

So, Like they always did on Easter Sunday, the neighborhood kids, each carrying their eggs, competed to see whose eggs were the strongest. They pointed the tops of their eggs at each other, as if they were swords, trying to smash them.

Laila too, was out playing with the neighborhood kids.

Noor gave her a few Easter eggs to participate in the game. And then Laila said, I can't wait to share with you our celebration for Eid El Fitr.

The neighborhood was just filled with joy, neighbors going from door to door offering their holiday greetings. The kids' excitement with eating Easter chocolate and cookies and smashing the colorful Easter eggs filled the place with laughter, love and the holiday spirit.

 **Wafa Shami,** was born and raised in Ramallah, Palestine. She Moved to the U.S. to pursue her education and graduated with a Master's degree in International Studies. Since moving to the U.S. Wafa has maintained her engagement in Middle Eastern issues. She was inspired to write this children's story after her son was born, who is currently 4 years old. In addition, to being busy raising her son, Wafa has a passion for cooking and has started a food blog, in which she is sharing her family's recipes. Wafa currently lives in California. Visit her blog at www palestineinadish.com for delicious recipes.

 **Shaima Farouki** is a Palestinian artist born in Jerusalem in 1988. A graduate of Friends School and currently lives in Ramallah. Holds a Bachelor degree from Birzeit University in Journalism and Social Sciences. Shaima' had a passion and deep interest for arts. Shaima' worked on her talent through practice and by attending several workshops to improve her drawing skills. She also participated in many group art exhibits in Ramallah. Shaima' currently works and sells individual paintings. Recently, she started teaching drawing classes for beginners. In addition, she works on illustrations to children story books.